YOUR BONES

AN INSIDE LOOK AT SKELETONS

Distributed to Schools and Libraries
in the United States by
ENCYCLOPAEDIA BRITANNICA EDUCATIONAL CORP.
310 S. Michigan Avenue
Chicago, Illinois 60604

Library of Congress Cataloging-in-Publication Data
Murray, Peter, 1952 Sept. 29-   .
Your Bones—An Inside Look At Skeletons / written by Peter Murray.
    p. cm.
Summary: Discusses the location and function of the
various bones that make up the human skeleton.
ISBN 0-89565-968-9
1. Human skeleton—Juvenile literature.
[1. Skeleton. 2. Bones.]
I. Title.
QM101.M87 1993   92-7460
611'.71—dc20   CIP / AC

YOUR BONES

AN INSIDE LOOK AT SKELETONS

Written by
Peter Murray

Illustrated by
Viki Woodworth

How Many Bones?

Two hundred and six.

That is how many bones you have inside your body.

Some of the bones are thick and straight, like the big bone that goes inside your thigh.

Other bones are flat and curved, like the ribs that protect your heart and lungs.

The bone we call the shoulder blade, or *scapula*, is shaped like the blade of a shovel.

The backbone, or *spine* is made up of thirty-three disc-shaped bones called vertebrae, which protect your spinal cord.

There are even three delicate bones deep inside your ear that are so small you could fit them all on your little fingernail. These tiny bones help you hear.

And there are a few bones that are really weird looking. This is the hip bone, or *pelvis*. It connects your legs to the rest of your body. You need it for dancing, running, sitting or hanging upside-down from a tree branch.

If you had all 206 bones piled up, you would have a big pile of bones.

But if they were put together right, you would have a skeleton.

Skeletons for Everybody

Most animals have some kind of skeleton.
Mammals like dogs, cats, monkeys, water
buffaloes and two-toed sloths have skeletons that
look very much like ours.

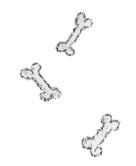

Birds have skeletons, and so do reptiles like lizards, snakes and crocodiles. Frogs and toads have skeletons, and fish have skeletons too. Some dinosaurs had the biggest skeletons of all.

All of these animals have skeletons inside their bodies, and all of them are built around the same basic plan: a spinal column made of *vertebrae*, a skull at one end, and a ribcage to protect the vital organs. This type of skeleton is called an *endoskeleton*, because it is inside the body.

Other animals have skeletons on the outside of their bodies. Clams have a skeleton made of only two "bones" and one joint. We call it a clam-shell, but to the clam it is a skeleton. Lobsters, crabs, and most insects have skeletons on the outside too. These outside skeletons are called *exoskeletons*.

The skeleton determines the shape of an animal's body. We can get an idea of what the original dinosaur looked like by looking at its skeleton.

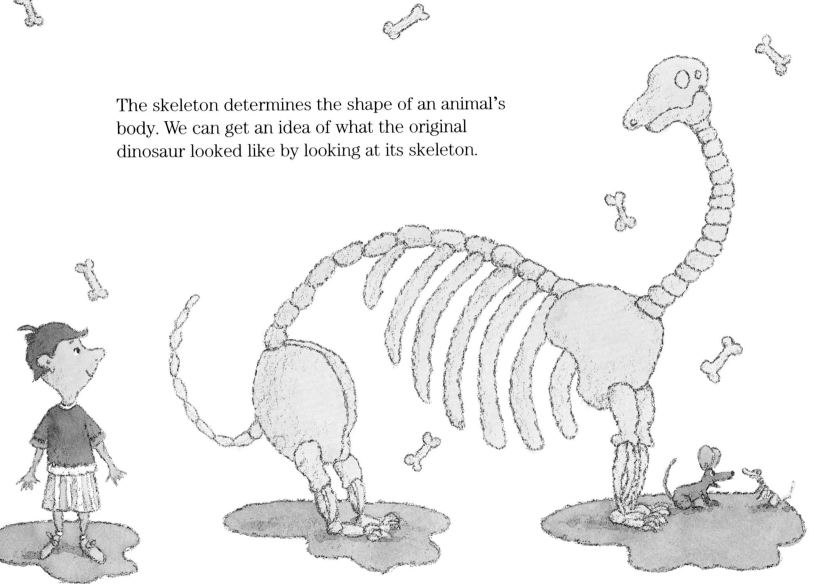

But a skeleton will not tell us the dinosaur's color.

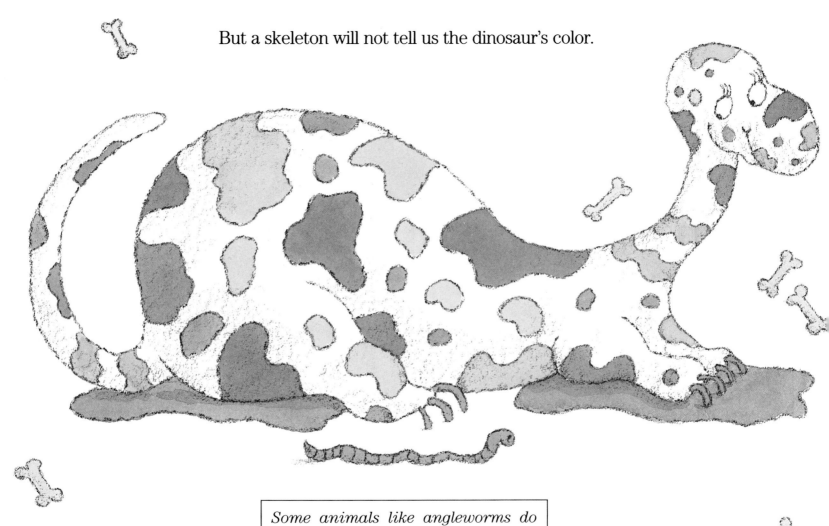

Some animals like angleworms do not have a hard skeleton. They never have to worry about broken bones!

16

Your Skeleton at Work

Skeletons do more than just give us our shape. They also provide anchors for our muscles so that we can move our bodies. If you did not have a skeleton, you would not be able to run, walk, or even crawl. You would have to ooze along on the ground like a big blob.

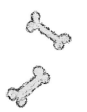

But, of course, you do have a skeleton. If you did not have one you could not read this because the muscles that move your eyes must attach to your skull. And you could not hear someone reading it to you, because you would not have the tiny bones that transmit sounds from your eardrum to your inner ear.

So unless you are a worm who can read, or an
intelligent amoeba from the Andromeda Galaxy,
you have a skeleton.

And you are using it right now.

Even when you are lying perfectly still on
your back with your eyes closed your skeleton
is working.

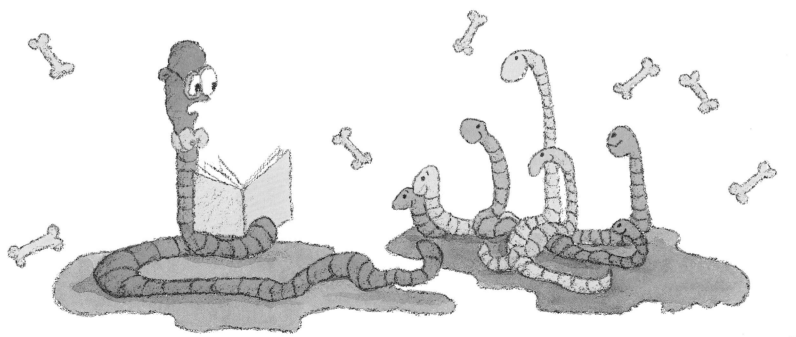

Living bones are not the hard, dry, brittle things
we see in museums. Your bones are alive and
growing and working every minute of the day.

On the inside of your bones there is a reddish, spongy tissue called *bone marrow*. Bone marrow makes your red and white blood cells. Every day your body uses up billions of blood cells, and every day your bones replace them.

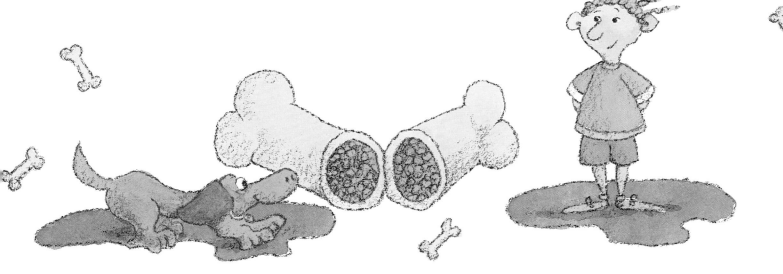

When a bone breaks, it can even heal itself. Doctors treat breaks by putting the broken limb in a cast or splint. This holds the parts of the bone in the right position so that they have time to grow back together.

Your Bones all Work Together

Because bone is so hard, we need more than one hundred movable joints so that we can change the shape of our bodies. If we did not have movable joints we would be like statues.

Our joints, where bone connects to bone, are held together with strong strap-like tissues called *ligaments*. The ends of the bones are protected by smooth pads of *cartilage*, which keep the bones from grinding against each other. And your muscles are attached to the bones by powerful, rope-like *tendons*.

When you lift this book, your bones, ligaments, cartilage, tendons, and muscles all work together to make it move. If any of these things were missing, lifting this book would be as difficult as trying to hold on to a 1000 pound weight.

Bones also store minerals such as calcium, magnesium, *and* carbonate. *These hard minerals, combined with a flexible material called* collagen, *give bones their amazing strength. Living bone is actually stronger than the same weight in steel or concrete.*

Uniquely Human

One of the unique features of the human skeleton is the size of the skull. Compared to overall body size, human skulls are the largest of any animal. This is because we humans have a lot of important stuff in our heads. (We also have a lot of not-so-important stuff, but our skull can't tell the difference.)

The main part of the skull is called the *cranium*, and it protects the brain. This large bone is actually made up of eight separate bones which grow together when we are very young.

The face of the skull is made up of fourteen bones. You can see that there is a hole where you would expect the nose to go. This is because your nose is made of cartilage, not bone.

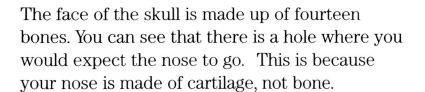

The bottom part of the skull is called the lower jaw, or *mandible*. It is the only part of the skull that can move. It goes up and down when you talk or eat. If it could not move, you would be very quiet and hungry.

Your skull is very thin, but very strong. You could test this by banging your head on the floor, but because you have such a big brain you probably know better.

The Complete System

All of the 206 bones in the human body are important. You need every one of the thirty-three bones in your spine. Even the smallest bone in your little finger has its job to do. Your skeleton is a system of bones, cartilage, and ligaments, all working together to help you do the things you want to do.

On the facing page is a picture of a human skeleton with the names of all the major bones. Notice that all the bones have a common name and a scientific name. The reason for the scientific names is so that doctors and scientists in every country can use the same names for the parts of the body.

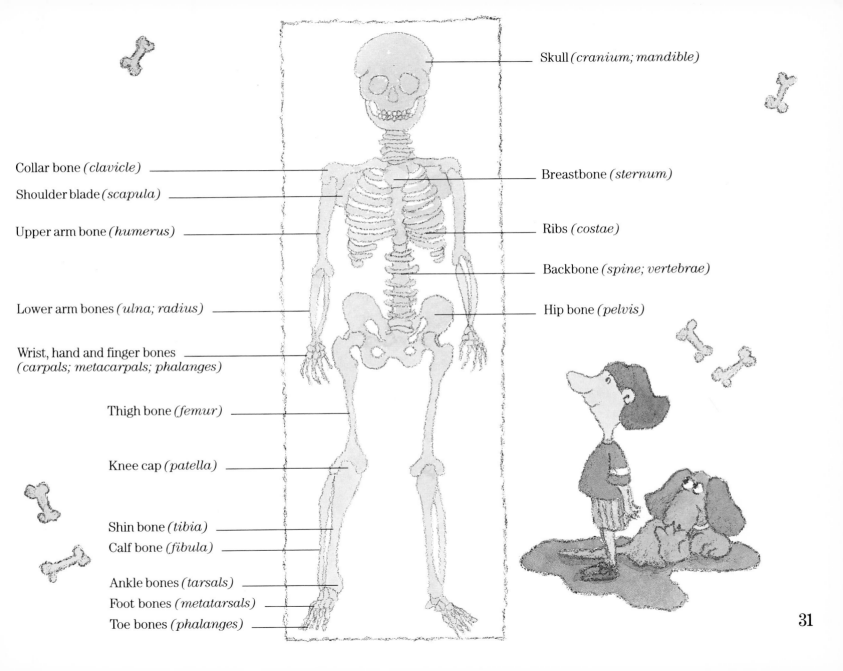

Skull *(cranium; mandible)*

Collar bone *(clavicle)*

Shoulder blade *(scapula)*

Breastbone *(sternum)*

Upper arm bone *(humerus)*

Ribs *(costae)*

Backbone *(spine; vertebrae)*

Lower arm bones *(ulna; radius)*

Hip bone *(pelvis)*

Wrist, hand and finger bones
(carpals; metacarpals; phalanges)

Thigh bone *(femur)*

Knee cap *(patella)*

Shin bone *(tibia)*

Calf bone *(fibula)*

Ankle bones *(tarsals)*

Foot bones *(metatarsals)*

Toe bones *(phalanges)*

31

611
MUR   Murray, Peter
                Your Bones- An
           Inside Look at Skeletons.

14.95

DATE   ISSUED TO

611   14.95
MUR   Murray, Peter
                Your Bones- An Inside
           Look at Skeletons.